Hat Making For Doll
1855–1916

Delineator
1883

Edited by Clare Blau

**Reprinted from the Old Books and Periodicals
in Our Collection with additional Patterns and Instructions
by Sandy Williams**

Published by **Hobby House Press** Hobby House Press, Inc.
Grantsville, Maryland 21536

Additional copies of this book may be purchased at $4.95 (plus postage and handling) from
Hobby House Press, Inc.
1 Corporate Drive
Grantsville, Maryland 21536
1-800-554-1447
or from your favorite bookstore or dealer.
©1979 by Hobby House Press
2nd Printing – 1982, 3rd Printing – 1991, 4th Printing – June 1994, 5th Printing – July 1996

ISBN: 0-87588-141-6

A Few Suggestions About Dolls' Hats.

For THE DOLL'S DRESSMAKER.

BY BROWNIE.

In looking over a few numbers of " THE DOLL'S DRESSMAKER," I found that nothing had been said in regard to head-wear. So, taking pity on poor dolly, I thought that I would contribute something on the subject.

When dolly is to be taken out for an airing she must needs have something to put on her head, in order to prevent her taking cold, as well as for adornment.

For instance, if it be a pleasant day in spring, then a dainty silk or wool hood or hat should be worn. A very pretty one can be made of pearl gray surah or china silk, with ribbons of the same color, or any other that the little mother may desire.

For a hat, a silk wire frame can be made or bought at some millinery store, then the silk is shirred on it, leaving a frill around the edge. Three rosettes of the ribbon make it prettier, and with ribbon strings—or not, just as suits Miss Dolly—the hat is completed.

For a hood, either silk or wool is suitable.

I think that dolly would make no objections to having one made of cream or white silk with dainty trimmings of lace and ribbon.

If the day be in June, then pretty straw hats and lace and embroidered hoods are worn. Take a white leghorn hat; line the under side of the brim with pipings of white silk or velvet; trim the outside with two or three of the tiniest of white feather tips and the hat is finished with some ribbon.

Another pretty one is made of tan colored lace straw, trimmed in cardinal ribbon, with a bunch of tiny red flowers. If dolly is a brunette, she will look charming in this.

But suppose the sky is clouded over and drops of rain begin to fall, and the little lady has not yet taken her exercise. What shall we do? If she goes out into the rain with one of her "pleasant-day"

hats, she will ruin it.

And she must be taken out for an airing, else she will be cross and sleepy. Therefore, the only thing that can be worn is a water-proof hat. Doubtless in the attic there is an old waterproof which Dolly's mamma has outgrown, and surely there is some part of it which is not too shabby to use. Now that we have found enough for the required hat, cut out a circular piece of the gossamer cloth and turn under enough for a small hem. Then above that make a small casing through which draw a rubber cord, fasten it together, and the cap is done. If it is puffed out it will take the form of a Tam O'Shanter. It would be nice if this could match her own waterproof.

Now that the pleasant days, and rainy ones too, have passed, winter is coming on. What shall she wear to keep her ears warm? There are many different kinds of caps and hoods, and in cases where dolly's ears are not at all tender, hats are preferred.

Some very pretty hoods are made of silk, wool or velvet, and some are crocheted of knitting silk and lined with the same shade of silk or satin. Ribbons generally trim them.

Caps are also made of different kinds of cloth. One very pretty one is a Tam O'Shanter. As to hats, some are felt and others are made of velvet.

I once saw one made of navy blue silk velvet, with trimmings of blue ribbon and one single long, white feather which was fastened in front with a bow of the ribbon and trailed around the side of the hat and fell a little below it on the hair. The effect was not only beautiful but striking indeed, as the dolly who wore it had golden tresses. One of seal brown felt, ornamented with a yellow and brown wing also some brown velvet ribbon, is another stylish hat.

Now that Dolly has a hat or two for every season, I think she will do very well.

In the making of these, one does not need to spend much time or money on them, for out of a few bits of silk or ribbon, some scraps of lace and parts of discarded feathers, very pretty jaunty hats and can be contrived in very little time.

About Measurements
1979 by Sandy Williams

Hats may fit doll's heads, or they may perch on top of the heads ("non-head-size"). "Non-head-size" hats are pinned to the doll's hair and will fit different sizes of dolls—the only "must" being that the hats are in proportion to the doll; the smaller the "non-head-size" hat, the smaller the actual doll's head size should be.

To measure a doll for a hat you need three measurements:

1). Obtain head size by measuring doll's head from center of forehead at hairline, around head, under bulge at back of head and then back to front.

2). Measure head from front to back.

3). Measure head from side to side.

These measurements can be utilized if one is drafting their own doll hat pattern.

In sewing hats for dolls, simplicity is important—the trims that look good on adult hats are most often overpowering on doll's hats. Trims must be in scale with the doll.

Use extra fine thread in sewing the hat together. Crinoline is a good hat stiffener; baste the crinoline to the hat fabric and treat as one fabric. Natural fabrics are the best to use: wool, 100% cotton, velveteen, silk, etc. Seam allowances are given in each hat's description; if not, add 3/16"– 1/4". Trim seams after sewing, clipping on curves and notching corners. Press after sewing each seam.

It keeps the hot sun from Miss Dolly's head— this garden hat trimmed with corn flowers

FROM WOMEN'S HOME COMPANION, JULY 1916

How to Trim a Hat.

An impression prevails extensively among ladies that the artistic decoration of a hat or bonnet can be properly designed only by those who have been regularly educated as milliners, or who may be gifted with a special and unusual aptitude for the business. To a certain extent this is undoubtedly true. Only a trained milliner can thoroughly understand the principles of the art, and tell at a glance what complexions, toilets, styles, trimmings, and colors, will blend together properly to produce a *tout ensemble* at once attractive, elegant, and harmonious. But, after all, this is only saying that a lady is not qualified to engage in business as a milliner without a previous special education. The fact remains, that a lady *can*, with a very little thought and study, learn what styles are best suited to her own individual features, complexion, and mode of dress ; and while she may be unable to trim hats or bonnets for her friends, she may do them for herself with as much taste and judgment as any milliner could display. Many a lady, who feels that she cannot afford the expense of a new bonnet, submits silently to the wearing of something that she knows is unsuited to her, in ignorance of the fact that, with a very trifling expense for material, and the exercise of a little patience and study, she might equip herself with a head covering which should excite admiration instead of pity.

As the hidden skeleton is that which gives its outlines to the body, so is the shape the primary factor in determining the style of a hat or bonnet ; and to the selection of a suitable shape, therefore, the first attention should be given. Shapes may be broadly divided into two general classes, high and low, the former being suited to ladies with long features and thin faces, while the latter are adapted to round, full faces. It may be noted also that long features require a *hat* to be worn drooping over the face, the English walking hat being the most becoming style ; but a *bonnet*, on the contrary, should be raised in front, to produce an effect of height which it would otherwise lack. Some shapes admit of much more trimming than others, and before making a final selection the style of trimming should be carefully considered and determined on.

The shape having been chosen, the next point to be considered is the trimming. This should be adapted not only to the style of shape, but to the age, complexion, and features of the wearer as well. Trimming may be classified as sober, medium, and gay, the first suitable for elderly ladies, the second for middle aged and married, and the last for young ladies and girls. A combination of the lighter shades of dark colors, as tan and brown, or silver gray and steel, may be relied on to produce a tasteful, sober effect. The medium trimmings should be of more decided shades, and are generally mixed with black ; very favorite combinations being of black with cardinal or cream-color, to which may be added flowers and feathers of the same colors. For young ladies, lighter and more pronounced colors should be employed, such as delicate shades of pink, sky blue, cream, white, etc., which are generally ornamented with flowers arranged in clusters, wreaths, and small bouquets.

Feathers should be selected of colors to match the materials used in trimming ; and in their arrangement upon the hat or bonnet there is room for the display of considerable taste, a carelessly draped feather usually ruining entirely the appearance of what would otherwise be a very jaunty and effective article of costume. A long feather should always be set in front of the crown, and drooped thence toward the back and side. Short feathers, on the contrary, should have a forward droop. The latter, when properly arranged, aid greatly in producing that coquettish effect in which so many young ladies delight. Wings and *pompons* also are serviceable in imparting a jaunty air. They should be worn at the side, and the angle at which they should be sloped is best determined by experiment in each individual case.

We advise every lady who may undertake her own millinery operations, to devote some time to practice in different styles, pinning the trimmings instead of sewing them, and noting the effect by the aid of her mirror. In this manner she will be apt to hit upon some very tasteful effects, such as, without experiment of this sort, she could never have designed. A bit of lace, or a few ribbons, are often a most effective ornament when rightly placed, and may be made to do service repeatedly for successive trimmings.

Harper's New Monthly Magazine
May 1855

The "Shape" or skeleton which we give below, will serve to show the general form of BONNETS, as they will be worn for the season. The trimmings, which give the special character to each specimen, are varied in ways almost infinite. We illustrate one composed of pink taffeta. The tabs, of the same material, together with the curtain, are bordered with straw braid. Drooping sprays of straw and crape buds form the outside trimming. In addition to these, the front has intermingled a *snow* of tulle and nœuds of pink ribbon. We observe that curtains cut in a point behind, and others open or slashed at the same place, are apparently coming into favor.

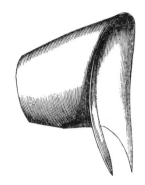

BONNET SHAPE.

BONNET.

Harper's New Monthly Magazine
May 1856

The BONNET SHAPES, from the latest Parisian models, will give a clear idea of their forms, without the aid of verbal description. It will be noted, among other variations from former styles, that the crown slopes more forward. These shapes are finished in almost every conceivable way, according to individual taste. The BONNET which we illustrate below is of white taffeta, traversed by bands of green crape, with a straw and feather braid at the front and crown and upon the curtain. The ribbons are of No. 6, green and white alternately. The strings are of No. 16, white taffeta. The ornaments are straw lilies of the valley and leaves, with blonde.

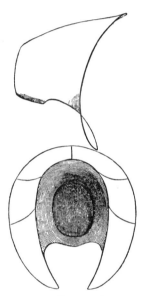

BONNET SHAPE.

BONNET.

Godey's Magazine   July 1860

We insert in our own department this cut of a bonnet, which is now all the rage. Everybody has it; men,

women, and children we were going to say, but we will leave out the first. It certainly is the most popular covering for the female head we have ever seen.

HAT (Fig. 1).—The shape may be made of black stiff net and black wire; cut it out as Fig. 2 for the crown, and cut through the four straight lines up to the dotted one, and bend the latter down; then make into a round by creasing the sides where they are cut through, and tack them together with black thread. Procure a piece of black silk velvet, and cut it the size of the round of Fig. 2, and it will form Fig. 3. For the brim, cut out of the same net the shape of Fig. 4, and cut out the round hole for the crown, and through the black lines at the top and bottom, turn up the dotted lines, and tack round inside of them a thin piece of wire, then fold over the top and bottom, where it is cut through, and sew the sides together. Cut a piece of black silk velvet on the cross, and shape it from the dotted lines to the circle in the middle of Fig. 4, and tack it under the brim of the hat; cut another strip of the same velvet on the cross, and bind the whole of the edge of the brim very neatly. Put in the crown, and fix it to the brim by sewing it all round, and the rough edge with a small piece of sarsnet ribbon, lining the inside of the crown with Persian silk, and it will form Fig. 5. Get a small white ostrich feather, rather long, and tack it inside of the brim on the top of the hat, carry it to the back, fasten it there, and allow

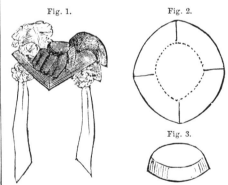

Fig. 1.   Fig. 2.

Fig. 3.

it to hang over a little. Cut some more strips of black silk velvet on the cross, and make up a nice large bow upon black net, and ends of the same; but before making

Fig. 4.

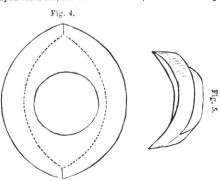

Fig. 5.

up the velvet, it should be hemmed all round. The strings must be pink ribbon; the rosettes can be made of pink and black velvet arranged upon black net.

Directions for Making Bonnet Frames and Bonnets.

WITH the aid of the accompanying figures, our readers will be enabled to make their own bonnet-frames, cheaply and easily, which will often prove a great convenience to those living in the country. We also give patterns of the latest styles of bonnets, which it is often difficult or impossible to obtain in small places.

Editor's Note:
These directions may be helpful for the doll's hat maker. Supplemental material on this page and page 7 (Figures 48, 49, 50, 52, 53, 56 and 57) not included.

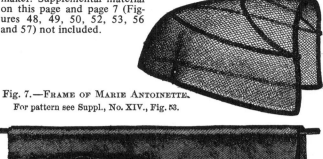

Fig. 7.—FRAME OF MARIE ANTOINETTE.
For pattern see Suppl., No. XIV., Fig. 53.

Fig. 1.—OUTER WIRE OF BONNET FRAME—REDUCED.

The making of a bonnet frame is very simple; the material needed is foundation muslin, coarse and fine wire, and, for some styles, also silk.

For the simple forms, shape first the outer edge of the frame of coarse wire, allowing the ends to lap over about an inch, and fastening them together as shown in Figs. 1 and 2, with fine wire such as is used in making flowers. Instead of this, fine bonnet-wire may be used, which is easily taken out. The so-formed wire circle (see Fig. 1), the size of which is according to the size and

Fig. 8.—MANNER OF MAKING BANDEAU FOR POMPADOUR—FULL SIZE.

Fig. 2.—JOINING OF THE WIRES—FULL SIZE.

Fig. 3.—WIRE OF BONNET FRAME—REDUCED.

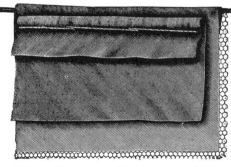

Fig. 9.—BINDING OF BONNET—FULL SIZE.

form of the frame, and is designated in the descriptions accompanying each, must now be bent into the requisite form as shown in the pattern accompanying each description. The ends which are fastened together must always come in the middle of the back of the frame. The cross wires, of fine wire, must next be fastened to this, as shown in the patterns and accompanying descriptions. Each of these pieces should be cut about half an inch longer than is given in the cut. The ends of these cross wires are wound around the outer edge of the frame-work as shown in Fig. 4. It is well to use scissors or a knife in order to make the fastening firm. The points where the wire crosses are fastened by means of threads, the ends of which are tied. Having finished the frame-work, stretch the foundation muslin lightly over it, fastening only on the outer border.

Fig. 4.—FASTENING OF CROSS WIRE TO THE OUTER WIRE OF FRAME—FULL SIZE.

For the frame of a black bonnet use black foundation and black wire, and for a white bonnet white material; for a lace or crape bonnet in colors wind the frame with narrow bias strips of

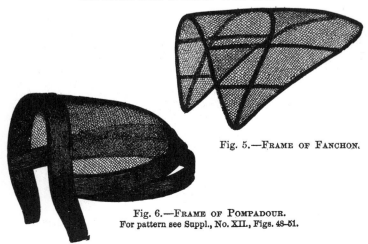

Fig. 5.—FRAME OF FANCHON.

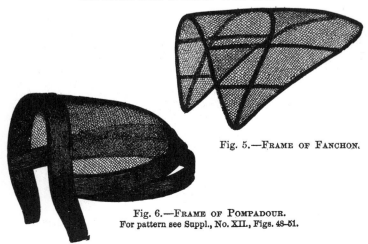

Fig. 6.—FRAME OF POMPADOUR.
For pattern see Suppl., No. XII., Figs. 48–51.

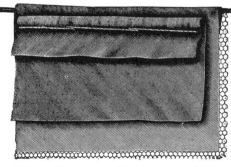

Fig. 10.—BINDING OF BONNET—FULL SIZE.

the same material, and cover the foundation with several thicknesses of the same, in order that it may not show through. Pliers are used for cutting the wire; if these are not at hand make an oblique cut with the scissors, after which it is easily broken.

The most simple style here given is the "Metternich," Fig. 5. In making the frame for this, fashion the outer part of the frame-work from a wire twenty-five inches long, after the pattern given in Fig. 52 of the Supplement, as shown in the illustration Fig. 1. The cross wires are placed as shown in Fig. 52 of the Supplement, and the accompanying illustrations Figs. 2–8. Over the prepared frame-work stretch tightly a piece of foundation, hem-stitch it over the outer wire, cut the edges away a quarter of an inch from the edge of the wire, and sew this down on the inside of the frame.

Fig. 7 is the Marie Antoinette. Begin this by fastening the ends of a wire twenty-four inches long in the manner shown by Fig. 2, bend it in the shape given by Fig. 53 of the Supplement, and fasten to this the middle long wire and the cross wires as shown by Figs. 3 and 4. On this lay the doubled stuff bias along the middle line, and cut the sides, leaving half an inch of the material beyond the edge. In the front part lay the pleat as shown above and sew the foundation to the outer wire. The Augusta bonnet is made after the same pattern as the Marie Antoinette.

The "Pompadour" bonnet, Fig. 6, consists of three bands and a head-piece of the foundation muslin. In forming this, cut first of any silk at hand—it is immaterial whether it be old or new—two bias bandeaux, each two and a half inches wide, the one eleven and the other twelve inches in length; in addition to these a straight piece of foundation muslin twelve and a half inches long, for the front band. The material of the bandeaux is to be laid over on both sides at the distance of three-fourths of an inch from the edge, so that each finished band shall be one inch wide. In each of the seams made by thus folding the material lay a fine wire and back-stitch it fast. The upper edge of the stuff may be laid under in a narrow hem and then hemmed to the under edge as shown by Fig. 8. In order to give the silk bands the shape shown by Figs. 48 and 49, Supplement, the outer side of the stuff must be stretched and the wire bent as shown in the pattern. The finished bandeaux are fastened together at the points designated by the numbers. Then cut according to Fig. 50, Supplement, a piece of foundation muslin, bias along the middle, and extending a quarter of an inch beyond the edges. This must be sewed to the bands on the under side, holding the material in as required between the numbers 56 and 57. The Pompadour and Watteau bonnets are made in this manner:

Having completed the frame, proceed to cover it with the material chosen.

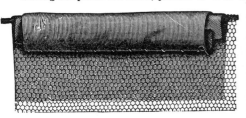

Fig. 11.—Binding of Bonnet—Full Size.

The manner of doing this, as also the arrangement of bows, flowers, lace, feathers, etc., can scarcely be described, but must be learned from illustration, and will depend on individual taste and the skill of the maker. It only remains to mention that the material must always be put on bias, so that it can be stretched at will, whether it be plain, pleated; or puffed over the frame. In putting on the outside material—if it be plain it must be tightly stretched—lay it over the frame, cut it at the distance of half an inch beyond the edge of the bonnet, and sew it fast to the foundation on the inner side, taking care not to let the stitches be visible on the outside. Line with tulle or material like the bonnet.

The borders may be made in different ways. Take either a piece of the bonnet material, or, in case that be light, of silk or velvet of the same color. Figs. 9–11 show a rounded border. Take a bias strip two inches wide, as shown by Fig. 9, and sew it on the bonnet, taking care to sew through the double material, and to draw the thread tight; lay the stuff over the edge and hem down on the under side so that the stitches shall not show on the outside.

The border shown by Fig. 12 is made in a similar manner, but in this a fold without a cord is laid on the right side. This may be of a different color from the bonnet.

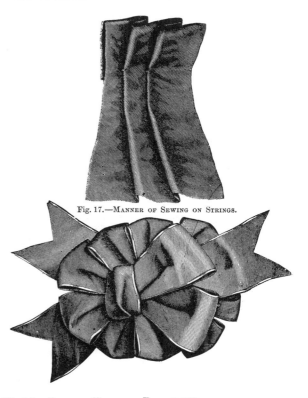

Fig. 17.—Manner of Sewing on Strings.

Fig. 18.—Rosette Bow for Pompadour—Half Size.

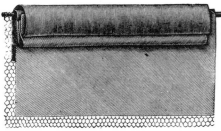

Fig. 12.—Binding of Bonnet—Full Size.

Fig. 13.—Bias Strip for Binding—Full Size.

Fig. 14.—Bandeau for Bonnet—Reduced.

Fig. 15.—Joining Wire for Bandeau.

Fig. 16.—Manner of Making Bandeau—Full Size.

Fig. 19.—Satin Bow for Trianon—Half Size.

Fig. 20.—Fan-Shaped Bow for Metternich—Half Size.

LADIES' POKE BONNET

FIGURE No. 1.—LADIES' POKE BONNET. The engraving shows the received style of poke for Winter wear. The truncated crown and enlarged brim make it differ somewhat from the one so well-known during the past year. The frame is smoothly covered with olive velvet, the under-facing being of the same material. A very long, full plume of shaded olive and pink is laid around the brim in the wreath fashion noted in old pictures. At the right side a curling tip is added as garniture. The strings are of broad, *ombré* ribbon, and their use is a mere matter of taste, as the bonnet may be worn as well without them.

FIGURE No. 1.—LADIES' POKE BONNET.

**VARIATION FROM THE DELINEATOR,
JANUARY 1882**

Additional Instructions
Fits about a 7" head size. Follow "Doll's Easter Hat" directions on page 17. Trim as pictured.

Poke Bonnet Crown

Hat Rim

Poke Bonnet Hat Band

↑sew to crown

←sew to Brim

LADY DOLLS' TURBAN

LADY DOLLS' TURBAN.—Velvet is used for the entire turban, which is in one piece and very easily made. After you have cut this piece out by the pattern, you will turn the lower edge under and then arrange it in three little upward-turning plaits, according to the instructions in the label and the notches and perforations in the pattern. The ends are now joined together, and then the end of their seam is brought backward and tacked to position, and back of this tacking two little backward-turning plaits are sewed in the seam. Another tacking is made in front of the first one, and the three upturning plaits first mentioned are tacked in their folds here and there to keep them in position. The becomingness of this dainty turban, when placed on Miss Dolly's head so as to show her crimps or bangs, is easily imagined; but then all little owners of dolls—and every little girl should have a doll—will want to see for herself how it really looks, and so they will make it up of plush, velvet, flannel, Surah or some other silk or woolen fabric. Usually such turbans will match the dress.

SET No. 86.—LADY DOLLS' LANGTRY COAT, TURBAN AND SHOPPING—BAG.

Editor's Note:
The pattern referred to in the description above is not shown. Please refer to the *Additional Instructions* to the right for further clarification.

Additional Instructions

The following instructions are for a doll's turban that will fit a 9-1/2" head size:

From velvet, cut a 7" circle for the crown, and a hatband measuring 3-7/8" x 10". Cut a 1-3/4" x 10" strip of silk to line the hatband. Use 1/4" seams. On the hatband, turn 1/4" of bottom seam in and then make three upward-turning pleats each 3/8" wide and 3/4" deep. Gather circle around edge and sew to top seam of hatband. Sew ends of hatband together. Tack pleats here and there in the folds to keep the pleats from coming undone. Sew hatband lining in so no raw seams are visible.

CHILD'S HAT

FIGURE No. 1.—CHILD'S HAT.—This picturesque hat will undoubtedly be very popular, for it is admirably suited to the small woman. It is of blue felt, with a broad binding of red velvet. On each side of the front are three broad red velvet ribbons, which are fastened to the crown by bronze ornaments that seem to pin them down. The ribbons are carried to the back and are there tied together in a profusion of loops and ends, the latter being quite long and having their edges notched. In brown, dark-green and gray these hats are obtaining.

FIGURE No. 1.—CHILD'S HAT.

Additional Instructions

Fits about a 7" head size. From crinoline, cut the Rim pattern, Hatband and Crown. Follow the "Doll's Easter Hat" directions (page 17) and sew a thin wire on outside edge of crinoline rim. Trim as desired.

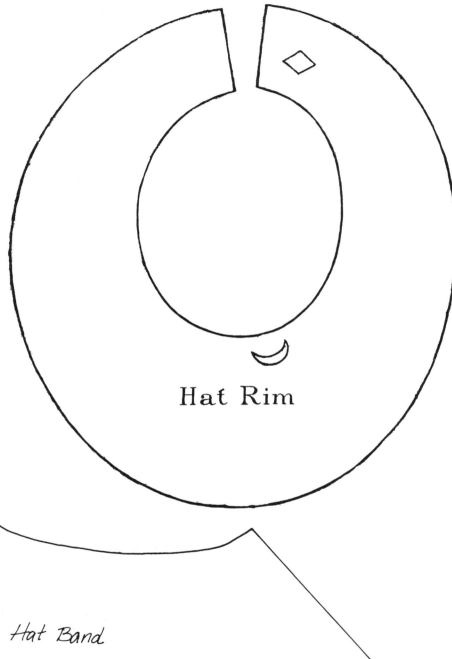

Hat Rim

1886 Child's Hat Crown

1886 Child's Hat Band

DOLL'S BONNET

No.XV. DOLL'S BONNET.—[See Illustration, Fig. 5, on page 860.]
Fig. 70 Half of Brim.
Fig. 71. Half of Crown.

This little bonnet is made of cream-colored satin and cream lace. Cut the brim of stiff net from Fig. 70; join it from 65 to 66, wire it at the edge, and cover it on both sides with pleated lace. Cut for the crown a double piece according to Fig. 71, of satin with white foundation for lining. Pleat it across the bottom by bringing X on ●, gather the edge from 67 to *, and join it to the brim from 67 to 68. Trim it with a band and bows of narrow feather-edged ribbon.

Fig. 5.—DOLL'S BONNET.—For pattern and description see Suppl., No. XV., Figs. 70 and 71.

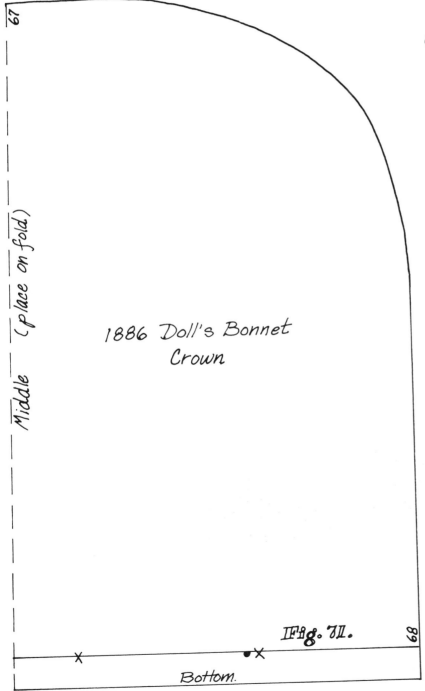

1886 Doll's Bonnet
Crown

Middle (place on fold)

Fig. 71.

Bottom.

67

68

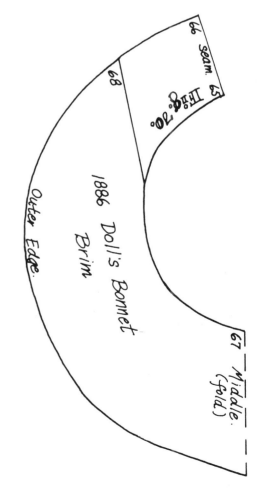

1886 Doll's Bonnet
Brim

Fig. 70.

Outer Edge.

66

seam.

65

68

67

Middle. (fold)

CHILD'S OUTDOOR TOILETTE

—CHILD'S OUTDOOR TOILETTE.—

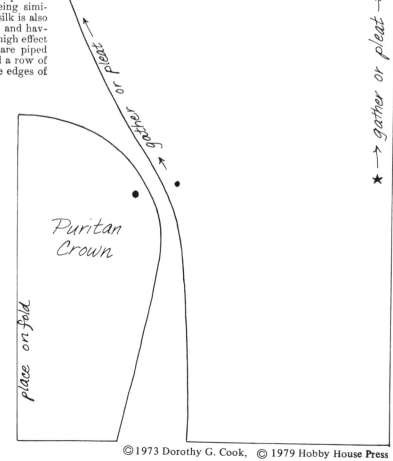

The cap has a plain crown-portion, and a full front that is made to stand picturesquely high by box-plaits in its front edge, side-plaits in its back edge and an interlining of crinoline, the crown being similarly interlined to give it the desired stiffness. A lining of silk is also added, that for the front fitting smoothly at its front edge and having only enough plaits in its back edge to fit nicely. The high effect desired in front is thus achieved. The edges of the cap are piped with the Surah and finished with a narrow frill of lace and a row of fancy stitching. A row of stitching is also made along the edges of the crown, at the bottom of which a ribbon bow is tacked. The ties are of ribbon and are bowed stiffly under the chin.

All sorts of dainty, soft materials will be made up into caps of this style, Surah, *crêpe*, mull, China and India silk, cashmere, nun's-vailing, etc., being liked. The ribbon will usually be the same color as the material, and any variety of lace may form the framing. Cordings, pipings or narrow bindings will usually finish the edges, and the stitching may be added or not, as preferred.

ADDITIONAL INSTRUCTIONS
Cut hat from Child's Outdoor Toilette Brim and Puritan Crown. Cut lining and crinoline from Puritan Crown and Puritan Brim. 1/4" Seams are included on all patterns. Gather or pleat Child's Outdoor Toilette Brim between dots to fit crown; sew together. Repeat between stars of brim to fit brim lining stars. Proceed with the "original" directions given above.

LITTLE GIRLS' BONNET

FIGURE No. 9.–LITTLE GIRLS' BONNET.–Blue velvet of a very dark shade was used for making this little bonnet, which is cut by pattern No. 1265, price 7d. or 15 cents. The crown is made in high puffed fashion, while the brim, which fits closely to the face, emphasizes the quaint air. Bands of ribbon folded over start from each side at the lower edge and meet just in the center, where they are arranged in a fancy bow resting against the high crown after the fashion of the loops on mamma's *chapeau*. A full *quille* of lace outlines the edges; and the ties are of ribbon.

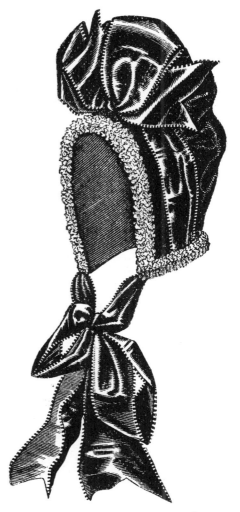

FIGURE No. 9.—LITTLE GIRLS' BONNET.—(Cut by Pattern No. 1265; 4 sizes; 2 to 8 years; price 7d. or 15 cents.)

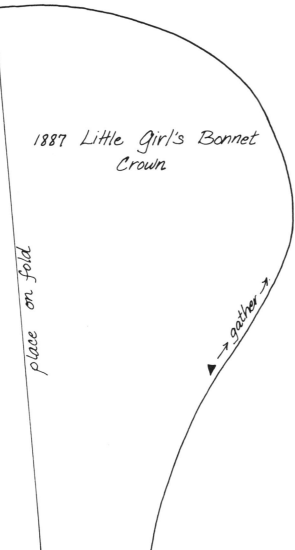

1887 Little Girl's Bonnet Crown

place on fold

→ gather →

Additional Instructions

Cut bonnet from Little Girls' Bonnet Crown shown here and Puritan Brim (shown on page 12). Cut lining and crinoline from Puritan Crown (shown on page 12) and Puritan Brim. 1/4" Seams included on patterns. Gather Little Girls' Bonnet Crown between triangles to fit brim; sew together. Line bonnet and trim as pictured.

FIGURE NO. 4.—CHILD'S HAT.

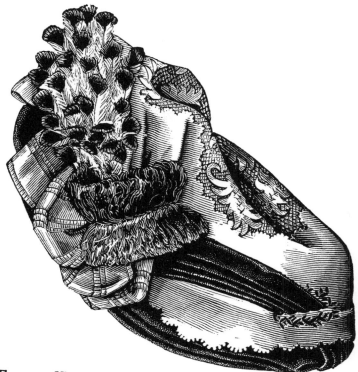

FIGURE No. 4.—LADIES' CLOTH AND VELVET *Toque.*

FIGURE No. 4.—CHILD'S HAT.—This pretty little sun-hat will find many admirers among mothers and will be liked in the nursery because of its comfort and simplicity.   It is of pretty, firm straw of a light tan shade, and the edge is finished with an extra braid, which renders binding unnecessary. Three bands of brown velvet ribbon are about the crown, and directly on top of it and well to the front are innumerable loops of mode grosgrain ribbon arranged so that some fall forward, while others, much longer, come over the brim in the back. Of course, ribbon of any color harmonizing with the costume may be used for trimming.

FIGURE No. 4.—LADIES' CLOTH AND VELVET *Toque.*—An elaborate *toque* adapted to dressy wear is here shown. The edge is finished with folds of golden-brown velvet, and the crown, which is formed of a pinked square of mode cloth, is elaborately embroidered in gold and green. Through the crown at one side a velvet strap is drawn to intensify the contrast. The garniture, which consists of loops of mode-and-brown ribbon, with a cluster of peacock's feathers resting against them, is placed on one side, a curious double band of feathers from the peacock's neck holding it in place.

The Delineator   July 1888

The Dolls' Dressmaker   August 1893

TAM O'SHANTER CAP

FIGURE No. 6.—TAM O'SHANTER CAP.—Dark-blue silk was used for making this jaunty cap, which is usually becoming to young faces. The full, soft crown is drawn in to a band made of folds of the silk, and is then bent over in a coquettish way. Two gold quills are arranged on one side as illustrated. These caps have the merit of being very becoming when they are so at all. They may be made of silk, velvet or any material suitable for a bonnet, so a harmony between the cap and gown is easily arranged.

BOY DOLL'S CAP.

Boy Doll's Cap.

This pretty cap may be made up in blue flannel. By stitching on the wrong side, close the seam at the front of the crown where you see the single notch, the seam at the back according to the double notches, and the seam at the sides according to the three notches. Then join the ends of the band, and sew its upper edge to the loose edge of the crown, right sides together, with its seam at the back seam of the crown. The finished size of the cap is approximately 3-1/2"-square with a head opening that measures approximately 2".

FIGURE NO. 6.—TAM O'SHANTER CAP.

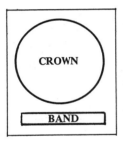

CROWN

BAND

Half the CROWN

FOLD

Half the BAND.

LADIES' WALKING HAT

FIGURE NO. 2. —LADIES' WALKING HAT.

FIGURE No. 2.—LADIES' WALKING HAT.—A very stylish shape is here represented in black chip. The outside of the brim, which rolls deeply at the sides, is covered with black Irish point lace, and the high crown is banded with wide black velvet ribbon disposed in flat loops in front, and a Rhine-stone buckle holds them in place. At the left side toward the back is an arrangement of long and short black Prince's tips. The hat is stylish, but somewhat severe in tone, though this may be modified by wearing a Tuxedo or other stylish face veil, which should reach quite to the chin.

VARIATION FROM THE DELINEATOR, DECEMBER 1881

FIGURE No. 2.—LADIES' WALKING HAT.

FIGURE No. 2.—LADIES' WALKING HAT.—An enlarged English walking hat is much in vogue this season. The one illustrated is of moleskin beaver in a dark gray shade. As usual, simplicity governs the quanity and style of the trimmings on such hats; though, just now, Dame Fashion allows on them more than she ever has before. At the left side, near the back, are two full tips of a dark gray color, and immediately in front is a bright-colored bird, poised so naturally that it looks as if just ready for flight. This hat is worn far over the face, the front hair not showing at all.

Hat Crown

An **EASTER** **HAT** for **DOLLS**

Hat Rim

Hat Band

Doll's Easter Hat.

This hat may be made from any material you have on hand, either silk or velvet.

First take the patterns and lay them on stiff piece of crinoline or wiggin. Then cut them out. These make the foundation, and must be covered with velvet or silk. The rim must be covered on both sides and the band and crown on one side only.

When they are nicely covered, take the band and sew it to the rim, but before doing this join the rim nicely in the back where you see the little perforation.

Then join the band to the rim, letting the crescent-shaped perforations come together.

When the band is nicely joined to the rim, take the crown piece and sew it to the band, placing the round perforation at the back of the hat. Now you have the little hat made, and I hope you have done it nicely.

Any pretty trimming will answer for it. You must use your own taste in that. The little crown may be strewn with fine pearls or any kinds of beads. Lace of any kind may be put around the band, or a pretty twist of ribbon may be placed around it, as you see it in the picture. A little bunch of violets or flowers of any sort placed in front look very pretty.

A piece of hat wire might be sewn on the outside edge of the crinoline rim before the covering is put on; this will enable you to bend the rim up nicely as shown in the picture, but the lining may be stiff enough without the wire; if so, you need not use it.

Doll's Hat.

This beautiful pattern for a doll's Christmas hat may be made up in black velvet and trimmed with pink rosettes and pink feathers. It is charming, and we hope many of our little readers will try to make it.

Lay the patterns on a stiff lining, and pin them down nicely; then cut them out carefully. When this is done, lay the patterns on the velvet, pin them down in

the same manner, and cut the velvet out, not forgetting to cut out two pieces of the velvet for the brim—one for covering and one for lining.

Cover the stiff lining with the velvet, and when each part is nicely covered join them all together. To form the hat's "indentation" gather from points A to point B. Trim with rosettes and ribbon according to taste.

DOLL'S HAT.

LITTLE GIRLS' PURITAN BONNET

No. 6679.—This pretty bonnet is shown made of velvet at figure No. 287 G in this magazine.

The bonnet possesses the simplicity and air of quaintness which characterizes the Puritan modes and is here shown made of camel's-hair and silk. It has a wide front that fits the head closely and is joined in a curving seam to an oval crown. Ornamental sections which are quite wide at the upper ends and narrowed at the lower ends are joined to the front edge of the front; they are lined with silk and stiffened, like the front and crown, with an interlining of crinoline; and their upper ends, which meet at the center, are wired and bent forward to present the effect of Valkyrie wings. To the lower edge of the bonnet is joined a curtain, which is shirred near the top to form a pretty frill-heading. The plaited ends of silk tie-strings are joined to the lower front corners of the bonnet and are prettily bowed; and a full ruching of narrow lace decorates the front edge and forms a pretty framing for the face. A silk lining consisting of a wide front and oval crown is added.

The bonnet will make up attractively in velvet, Bengaline, corded silk, cloth, cashmere, and various other silks and woollens, and may be trimmed with embroidery, feather-stitching, ribbon, etc.

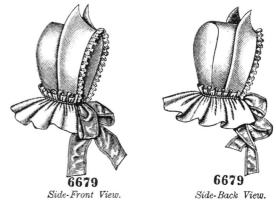

6679
Side-Front View.   **6679**
                              Side-Back View.

LITTLE GIRLS' PURITAN BONNET. (COPYRIGHT.)

Additional Instructions

Follow "original" directions above and use 1/4" seams. If you wish to sew a "curtain" around the bottom edge of the bonnet, cut the "curtain" 1-3/4" x 12-1/2"; narrowly hem one long edge and the two short edges; turn raw edge in 3/8" and gather 1/4" from edge to fit bonnet; sew "curtain" to bonnet.

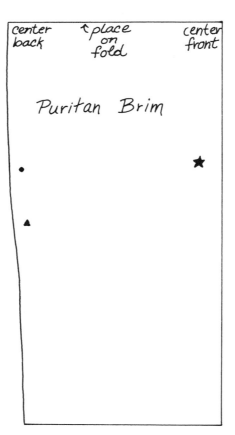

Puritan Bonnet
Valkyrie Wing

center back   ↑ place on fold   center front

Puritan Brim

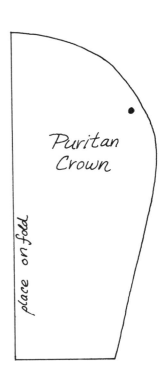

Puritan Crown

place on fold

EMPLOYMENTS FOR WOMEN.—No. 6.

MILLINERY.

THERE are several weighty reasons which recommend the milliner's trade to the girl who is casting about for a means of support. In the first place, it is essentially feminine. Because of that quality, and also because men are usually lacking in the delicacy of touch which is necessary to the proper handling of frail materials, there is comparatively little rivalry between men and women in this avocation. This statement is qualified advisedly, for we all know that there are men engaged in the work, and that a few firms prefer them to women as trimmers, arguing that they are bolder and more original in designing. These cases, however, are so rare as to be the exceptions that prove the rule. We speak of a man-milliner, never of a woman-milliner, because the craft belongs inherently to women, just as tailoring does to men. The question of woman suffrage over which we have all been either sharpening our wits or losing them, has emphasized the fact that in whatever pursuit man's efforts are pitted against woman's, the man usually makes the more money. Why this should be so is a query which cannot be entered into here; but the fact being incontrovertible, we must conclude that any business in which we are able to engage with the least chance of opposition is likely to afford the best results.

Again, the materials used in constructing or embellishing a hat are not cumbrous, so there is no heavy weight to strain the muscles or tire a weak back. Moreover, no unhealthy fumes arise to penetrate the lungs, nor does the handling of the fabrics entail a steady, cramped position. The work can be as well and as speedily done at home as in a shop. Indeed, there are more than a few women who earn comfortable incomes by making head-gear for regular customers, and at the same time find no difficulty in attending to their domestic duties, although they may be mothers of young children. It is this convenience of work to hand that differentiates the task of the milliner from that of any other toiler save the dressmaker.

The usual remuneration for such employment is frequently increased by a percentage which the worker is allowed at the shops where she makes her purchases. She often buys a hat and all its trimmings, and certain firms give her a discount, which, of course, is a legitimate addition to her regular pay. There are others who make a fair living by going out by the day as seamstresses do They charge a fixed amount for a day's work, which may include the originating of a new hat, the copying of a French pattern, or the "doing over" of last season's *chapeaux*—usually the last. But by far the greatest advantage of the millinery trade is its adaptability to all sorts and conditions of women. Those who have been deprived by circumstances of a fair share of education may become as skilful at it as their more fortunate sisters, for it is one of the few avocations for women in which a lack of book-knowledge is not a serious drawback.

Let us see what qualifications are necessary for success. It should first be stated that there are two branches of the trade. The public at large defines the word "milliner" as meaning a person who makes hats or bonnets, but inside the circle of the initiated there are milliners and trimmers, and there is a difference between them in the matter of salary of from fifteen to twenty or thirty dollars a week. The position of a trimmer is the highest grade attainable, and to reach that coveted place one must possess a faculty which is born in some, and which is known as "style." Almost all women can become milliners, but those who have not genius will never make good trimmers. They may be successful at copying, but they can never originate. The milliner prepares the hat or bonnet for the trimmer. The facing, folds or covering is first placed, and after all tedious preliminaries are completed and a good foundation secured, the trimmer adds the superstructure, which may be more or less ornamental, but is always stylish.

Only firms that cater to the most fashionable trade employ trimmers, so called. In most cases these artists are imported, like sample hats, from Paris, and they command excellent salaries, forty dollars a week being about the average, although some receive as much as fifty or even sixty. There are millinery establishments in New York, however, which are patronized by the best class of customers, and which are nevertheless strictly American in their work. The writer has particularly in mind one very exclusive house which imports many things, but not employes. All of its work is done by American women, whose training begins when they are children. They enter the house as errand and general utility girls at eight dollars a month, and grow up with the business, their salaries keeping pace with their proficiency. Some of them turn out skilful trimmers, and the others are certain to become good milliners. The latter are paid twenty dollars a week, the former twenty-five or thirty. Of course, there are many firms that do not aim to secure the most exacting trade, and who, therefore, do not make much distinction between milliners and trimmers. With them every milliner is her own trimmer, with a result satisfactory to all concerned. Salaries in such cases are below the figures quoted. fifteen dollars a week being considered good remuneration.

After "style," the attribute most necessary to make a successful milliner is neatness. By this is not meant the faculty which leads to a rigid management of one's bureau-drawers, but the greatest nicety in stitching and the utmost delicacy in handling materials. I have known girls who would be oblivious to dust in a room and would be indifferent to an interchange of places between a paper of pins and a prayer-book, but who could for all that do exquisitely dainty work with the needle.

If I have given anyone the impression that the millinery trade is a mere trifle to learn, or a sinecure to practise after having been learned, such was far from my intention. In placing before the reader its advantages, I do not wish to be misleading. Salaries are good compared with those paid in many other employments offered to women, but dull times must be considered. There are two seasons, the Autumn, comprising about three months, and the Spring, about four. Trimmers are usually engaged by the year, but milliners only by the season. Thus the milliner has work during only seven or, allowing a margin, eight months in the year, and must remain idle during the balance of her time.

There is no occupation which requires more patience than hat and bonnet making. Every stitch must be accurately placed, and a piece of velvet may be ruined by the careless pressure of a finger. Suppose we go through the process of trimming a hat; that will illustrate my point better than anything else. We must choose a simple one, because the limits of a single article cannot embrace the

whole science of millinery, nor must the beginner attempt too great a task at the start. We will take a black straw, which is always a safe investment. It looks well with any kind of a toilette, and it may be trimmed with anything. We must not involve ourselves too much in the subject of color, for that would be more than we could manage just now. We will, then, select a rough-and-ready black straw, with a low, round crown and a moderately wide brim. The latter is very narrow at the back and turned up slightly, and in front there is a decided peak, which is a necessary feature, since the woman who is to wear the hat has a round face and needs a high arrangement above her forehead to lessen the appearance of width.

Our customer does not wish too sombre a head-covering, so we measure about the extreme edge of the hat brim, and finding the circumference thirty-four inches, we buy that length of cream-colored straw edging, with half a yard extra for a purpose to be explained later, and also three-quarters of a yard of black moiré. All silks and velvets for millinery work should be bias, but moiré is not cut bias in the shops, and we must take what we can get. Next we select two bunches of roses and buds, six in each, the flowers shading from delicate pink to a deep crimson; for our patron is quite pale and finds that red upon her hats casts a faint glow of color upon her face. Being supplied with a paper of milliner's needles, assorted from five to ten, we procure black ribbon wire, which is sold by the piece, black cotton-covered wire, heavy black silk covered wire, also in the piece, and a spool of Kerr's thread, letter D. This last is a valuable addition to the work-basket of any woman; it is highly glazed and does not snarl, and it is obtainable in black only, being wound on large spools. This thread must take the place of silk in every part of the hat where it can possibly be used. Then we must have a box of round-headed black pins, because they are so much sharper than any other kind that they readily penetrate the most obstinate substance, and leave no mark when withdrawn; and next on our list is lining silk. It is economy to buy three-quarters of a yard of the silk, which will make three linings and will cost less than three linings that have been prepared in the shop. A small piece of buckram is needed, and as the material is always useful, we will take half a yard of it, black, of course. Half a yard of black baby ribbon or the same quantity of taste completes our purchases.

Now to work. Every hat must have wire about the edge. Most shapes have this wire when purchased, and the one we have selected is thus provided, but the wire is cotton-covered and will not answer our purpose; and, besides, it must be ripped off to admit of sewing on the white straw. Taking a pair of sharp scissors, we insert the flatter blade between the wire and the hat and press gently against the thread which connects them, and in a second it is severed all the way round, with the cut ends clinging to the wire. We first sew the straw edge about the hat, beginning at the back, where the joining will be covered by trimming. We hold the under side of the hat toward us and keep the edge of the white straw even with the edge of the hat, as we do not wish too much of it to be visible on top. The sewing is done with the cotton thread, and we take a

short back-stitch on top and a long forward one on the under side of the brim along the heading of the straw edge we are sewing on. The straw must be held in slightly along its inner edge so it will lie flatly along the outside, and an inch and a half must be allowed for joining and securely fastening the ends one on top of the other, to prevent them from ravelling.

As the hat measures thirty-four inches round, we cut off a piece of the silk-covered wire thirty-five inches and a half long, the extra inch and a half being allowed for joining. If you should contemplate doing much work of this kind, it would pay to buy a pair of wire cutters, which are inexpensive and will save much rough wear upon the scissors. Fortunately for us, silk wire is popular this season and causes a great saving of labor, for although it is hard to sew on, the work is easier than making a covering for cotton wire. Beginning at one end of the wire, after threading the needle, we knot the thread, draw it through the casing of the wire, and wrap it tightly round the wire about half an inch from the end to keep the covering from ravelling and slipping off. We now leave the needle fast, and, beginning at the back of the hat and holding the under side of the brim toward us, place the wire on the head of the straw edge so as to cover the line of sewing previously made. We take a long forward stitch, inserting the needle in the under casing of the wire, and running it through to the right or upper side of the brim; then we take a short back-stitch, bringing the needle out below the wire again; and so the sewing is continued. When we reach the starting point, we wrap the second end of the wire as we did the first, push it under the latter and sew it firmly.

We are now ready to trim the hat. First we place the silk right side up on a table and fold one corner over on top until the edge running across is at right angles with the edge of the main piece. We must be careful that the twill on the wrong side of the silk runs at right angles with the bias edge which we are to cut, for if it did not, the bias would not be true and we would have to take the other corner. Having cut the silk down the fold, we make two strips nine inches wide, cut off the white selvedge, join the strips, turn the edge over upon the wrong side three-quarters of an inch, and hem it by taking a stitch first in the body of the goods and then in the turn. Next we form the strip into two loops of equal length, inserting the ribbon wire; and these we place on the back of the hat, sewing them firmly against the side of the crown and making the cross-piece of silk and the surplus straw edge. Then we place the roses close together around the front of the crown, and sew a spray of them on the back to hide joinings and droop over the hair.

The next step is to cut a slightly crescent-shaped piece of buckram seven-eighths of an inch wide at the middle and six inches long, and wire it around the edge with cotton wire, using a button-hole stitch to keep the wire exactly at the edge. This section we cover with a piece of bias silk, overcasting it on the upper, concave edge, and then place it on the hat in front, with the widest edge out. The lining must be cut lengthwise of the silk, and must be hemmed on one edge deep enough to allow the taste to be run through; and we measure from the head size to the middle of the crown for its width, and around the head size and one inch extra for its length. This we sew in half an inch above the head size, beginning at the back and taking a long forward and short back stitch; and before drawing it up we place a rose on the piece of false crown under the peak in front, sewing it so that the stitches will be under the lining. Now we sew a small square of silk upon the inner tip of the crown, draw the ribbon in the hem of the lining, tie it in a small bow and run the overlapping ends together, and our hat is finished.

L. M. BABCOCK.

FROM THE DELINEATOR, APRIL 1892

LITTLE GIRLS' HAT 9153

9153

Instructions For 9153

Use 1/4" seams.

For the crown: Cut a strip of organdy 4" x 20". To make the "tuck casings" for the wires, turn up 1/4" along one edge of 20" side of crown; top-stitch 1/8" in from edge; make a tuck 1/4" deep and 1/8" apart from first casing. Sew the two 4" edges of crown together. Tightly gather the remaining 20" edge, pulling the raw edges to wrong side of crown. To make the "button mould," cover a 1/4" cardboard circle with several 3/8" circles of organdy. Cut two 9-1/2" lengths of thin, flexible wire. Make a small loop at each end of wire; insert wires into casings at seam; shirr crown until wire loops meet; tack loops to crown.

For the "lace-edged frill": Cut a strip of organdy 2" x 22". Turn up 1/8" along one edge of 22" side; top-stitch 1/4"-wide white lace over this edge. Cut organdy 3/4" away from lace edge and insert 1/4"-wide white lace. Seam 2" edges together.

For the brim: Cut a strip of organdy 4" x 22". Seam 4" edges together; turn right side out. Fold strip in half lengthwise; press. Top-stitch 1/8" in from folded edge to form a casing. Lay frill over brim; turn all raw edges of frill and brim in 1/4" to wrong side of brim; top-stitch close to edge and 1/8" in to form another casing. Insert a 22" length of wire into folded edge of brim casing; sew looped ends of wire to seam. Insert and shirr a 9-1/2" length of wire into other casing. Blind-stitch crown and brim together along 9-1/2" edges. Trim and bend brim wire as pictured.

9154   9154

LITTLE GIRLS' BONNET 9154

No. 9154.—A picturesque little bonnet, known as the Miss Muffet bonnet, is here illustrated made of light-blue piqué, white embroidered edging and insertion. The front fits the head closely and is joined to a circular crown, the ends being joined in a short seam at the center of the back. Joined to the front edges of the bonnet and flaring becomingly over the face are two frills of embroidered edging that are deepest at the center and narrowed gradually toward the ends; a similar frill falls from the lower edge of the bonnet, forming a curtain. A frill of narrow edging is set underneath along the joining of the deep frills and a similar frill is included in the seam joining the front and crown. The plaited ends of the tie-strings are tacked to the corners of the bonnet, and ribbon is arranged over the edges of the frills as a decoration.

ADDITIONAL INSTRUCTIONS 9154

Use 1/4" seams. Sew center back seams of Brim together. Sew Crown to Brim. Follow "original" directions above to complete bonnet.

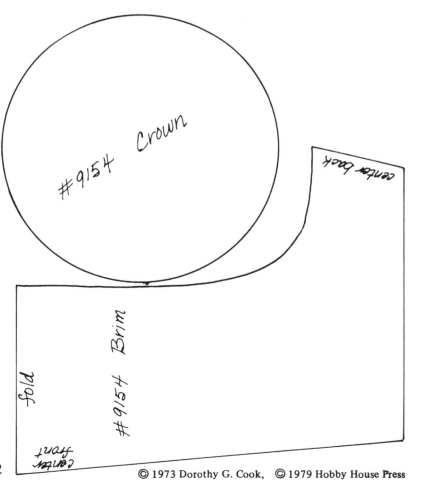

#9154 Crown

center back

Fold

#9154 Brim

center front

THE LITTLE HOUSEKEEPER

The March winds are so bad for Miss Dollykins' hair that it is quite essential that she should have a hood or cap to wear instead of a hat. For certain occasions it is well enough to have a hood fastened to the top of a golf cape, but the most stylish cap this spring is modeled on the head dress of a Dutch peasant, probably in compliment to the new little queen in Holland. These little caps are extremely pretty, and the Doll's Dressmaker will find them very easy to make.

Pieces of silk or velvet or some bright woolen material can be used in their construction, and a pattern is not at all necessary.

The way to take the first measure is this: Lay the customer for whom the cap is intended on a table with the back of her head on a piece of paper; holding a lead pencil upright, draw a line from just below one ear around the top of the head to just below the other ear. This will give the shape for the back of the cap. Cut this out of a piece of velvet and bind the round edge with a narrow strip of silk, so that it will not ravel. Then measure from the upper part of the back of the head to the top of the forehead. Take a strip of silk or a ribbon twice as wide as this measure and as long as the round edge of the velvet. Overcast one edge of this ribbon on to the round edge of the velvet back, and hem the lower straight edge of the velvet and the two ends of the ribbon with a very narrow little hem. Try the cap on to the customer and turn the front piece back not quite half way, but so that it will come just over her hair. At the two lower edges of this fold sew narrow ribbons to tie under the chin. The fold that is turned back must be left loose and soft. Of course these caps can be lined, but a lining is always a troublesome affair, and while March is blustering it is not cold, so the little mothers will find that their children are very comfortable with just a single thickness of cloth over their heads.

Dutch Cap Crown

DOLLS' DUTCH CAP

A LITTLE DUTCH CAP.

Additional Instructions

Use 1/4" seams. Cut two Crowns and a strip of fabric 7" x 9" for the brim. With right sides together, fold strip in half lenthwise; sew each end together; turn right-side-out. Turn neck edge up on wrong side of Crown. Pin raw edge of brim around Crown; sew together. Baste Crown lining in so no raw seams are visible. Fold brim back almost halfway as illustrated. Sew 1/2" wide satin ribbon ties at two lower edges of fold.

Infant Dolls' Set 5410

Girl Dolls' Dutch Set 5920

Boy Dolls' Dutch Set 5920

VARIATION FROM PICTORIAL REVIEW, DECEMBER 1914

1616   1616
Little Girls' Poke Bonnet. Ages, 2 to 8 yrs., 4 sizes. For 6 yrs. ¾ yd. 22 ins. wide, with ¾ yd. of Liberty silk for the poke lining. Price, 5d. or 10 cents.

1521
Little Girls' Bonnet. Ages, 3 to 7 yrs., 3 sizes. For 5 yrs., 1 yd. 22 ins. wide, with 1¼ yd. edging 5½ ins. wide. Price, 5d. or 10 cents.

1664   1664
Little Girls' Bonnet. Ages, 1 to 7 yrs., 4 sizes. For 5 yrs., 1¾ yd. 22 ins. wide. Price, 5d. or 10 cents.

9154   9154
Little Girls' Bonnet. Ages. 1 to 7 yrs., 4 sizes. For 5 yrs., 1½ yd. 22 ins. wide. Price, 5d. or 10 cents.

8710   8710
Little Girls' Bonnet or Hood. Ages. 1 to 9 yrs., 5 sizes. For 5 yrs., ⅝ yd. 20 ins. wide, with ⅜ yd. silk. Price 5d. or 10 cents.

847
Rob Roy Cap. Cap sizes 6 to 7½; or, head meas., 19¼ to 23¾ inches, 7 sizes. For cap size, 6¼, or head meas., 20 ins. ⅝ yd. Rob Roy plaid cloth 54 ins. wide. Price, 5d. or 10 cents.

1615   1615
Child's Bonnet or Hood. Ages, 1 to 7 yrs, 4 sizes. For 5 yrs. 1 yd. 22 ins. wide, with ⅛ yd. of velvet for covering the reversed portion, and ¾ yd. of lining silk. Price, 5d. or 10 cents.

8782
Little Girls' Bonnet. Ages, 1 to 7 yrs., 4 sizes. For 5 years, ⅝ yd. 22 ins. wide. Price, 5d. or 10 cents.

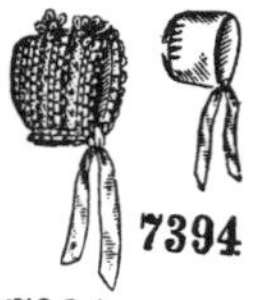

7394
Infants' Cap. One size. ¼ yd. 17 or more ins. wide. Price, 5d. or 10 cents.

6287
Infants' Cap One size. ⅝ yd. 20 ins. wide. Price, 5d. or 10 cents.

1017
Infants' Cap. One size. ⅞ yd. 20 ins. wide. Price, 5d. or 10 cents.

1848
Infants' Cap. One size. ½ yd. 20 ins. wide. Price, 5d. or 10 cents.

6075   6075
Cap, with Hexagonal Crown. Cap sizes, 6 to 6¾; or head meas., 19¼ to 21½ ins., 7 sizes. For cap size, 6½; or head meas., 20¾ ins. ¾ yd. 20 ins. wide. Price, 5d. or 10 cts.

3033   3033
Tam O'Shanter or Sailor Cap. Cap sizes, 6 to 6¾; or head meas., 19¼ to 21½ ins., 7 sizes. For cap size, 6½; or head meas., 19⅝ ins.. ⅝ yd. 20 ins. wide. Price, 5d. or 10 cents.

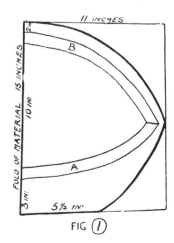

1481   1481
Little Boys' French Hat. Ages, 1 to 4 yrs., 4 sizes. For 2 yrs., ¾ yd. 22 ins. wide, with 1¾ yd. ribbon 2½ ins. wide for the ties. Price, 5d. or 10 cents.

4393   4393
Cap, with Square Crown. Cap sizes, 6 to 6¾; or head meas., 19¼ to 21½ ins. 7 sizes. For cap size, 6½, head meas., 20¾ ins. ⅝ yd. 20 ins. wide. Price, 5d. or 10 cts.

3167
Polo or Travelling Cap. Cap sizes, 6¼ to 7½, 6 sizes. For cap size 6¾, ⅜ yd. 27 ins. wide. Price, 5d. or 10 cents.

3166
Cap, for Outdoor Sports. Cap sizes, 6¼ to 7½, 6 sizes. For cap size, 6¾, or head meas., 21½ ins., ⅜ yd. 27 ins. wide. Price, 5d. or 10 cents.

DOLLS' PATTERNS.

The Materials Stated are for Dolls 22 Inches Tall.

Girl Dolls' Set No. 216.—Consisting of a Russian Blouse Dress and Brownie Bonnet. 14 to 28 ins. long, 8 sizes. 1⅝ yd. 22 ins. wide. Price, 7d. or 15 cents.

The Girl's Own Paper   Circa 1896

CHILD'S WASHING HOOD.

THIS charming little pattern fits so prettily on the head, is of very simple construction, and just the thing for garden or beach.

A small piece of washing material suffices, as will be seen from the measurements given in Fig. 1. A and B are merely soft twilled tape laid on and stitched at each edge to contain the runners of narrow tape, see Fig. 2, which shows the right side of the hood, the dotted lines indicating the stitching of the tape showing through from the wrong side.

There is a half-inch hem all round the hood, and the strings should be of ribbon, one yard, easily removed for washing.

One yard of embroidery is required for the edge, just eased on to set comfortably; one yard and a half of lace forms an inside frill stitched three-quarters of an inch further in than the embroidery.

If this frill is put on before the tape for the runners, the latter can be laid over the raw edges with a neat result.

"COUSIN LIL."

FIG ①

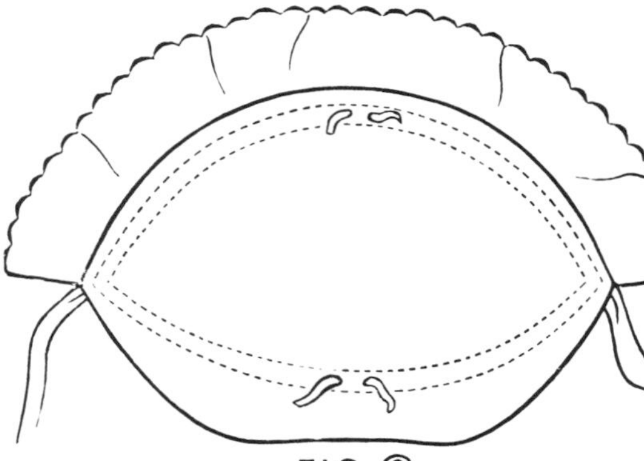

FIG ②

FIG ③

Late Autumn Millinery

MAKING A BONNET

BY AN EXPERT

THE bonnets worn at the present time by elderly and middle-aged ladies are really nothing more than small toques. They may be worn with or without strings, just as may suit the wearer.

The materials required to make the bonnet illustrated this month are: One-half yard of white mousseline de soie for covering the frame, one strip of fancy jet and chenille seven-eighths of a yard in length and five inches in width, two yards of white maline, one-half yard of black velvet, one and one-quarter yards of cream white satin antique ribbon, one white and three small black ostrich tips, and three medium-sized bright jet ornaments.

It must be kept in mind that it is most essential that a bonnet should fit comfortably on the head, consequently special attention should be given to the making of the frame.

To make the frame illustrated by Figure I, commence with the head wire; for this cut a piece of shirring wire twenty-seven inches in length, lap until it measures twenty-two inches, then fasten the two ends very firmly by winding them with the tie wire. Next bend this head wire up in a deep curve for the back of the bonnet and down at the front and sides. Figure I shows clearly how the wire should be curved. Next cut three pieces of wire about fifteen inches in length; take one of these for the wire which extends from front to back. Allow about five inches of the wire at one end to help form the coronet, then, using the pinchers, make a decided bend up for the crown. Fasten this wire very securely to the head wire;

FIGURE II

then measure six and three-quarters inches across the crown, at which point twist the wire around the head wire directly at the back and cut off the superfluous wire. Be careful to see that both sides of the crown measure exactly the same and that it is also sufficiently deep. Next adjust the two cross wires; these wires both measure six and three-eighths inches across the crown. Fasten them to the head wire, measuring from the front, to form the following spaces, three and one-half two and one-half and five inches Bend all the crown wires in the required shape so that the crown

will not be too shallow, as a bonnet especially should set firmly on the head. Tie all the intersecting wires together in the centre of the crown. In order to complete the crown, three wires should now be fastened around it. Next bend all the outward wires up to form the coronet; measure three and one-quarter inches for the height of the crown in front, three inches for the sides and one and three-quarters inches for the side-back. The coronet wire measures twenty-two and one-half inches. Begin at the front and fasten the upward wires to the coronet wire to form the following spaces: five, three and three-quarters and two inches. The space from the direct back of the frame to the end of the coronet measures four inches. Another wire fastens round and completes the brim. Curve in the coronet at both sides and the frame is ready for the covering. This is of double white mousseline de soie, plaited to make it smooth. Next, tack the white maline in soft, loose folds around the frame. Three widths of the maline will be required to pad out the coronet, while one width will do for the back. The fancy strip of jet and chenille should now be arranged over the maline. In doing this, allow much more fulness in front than in the back. Sew, with a few long stitches, one side of the strip to the top of the coronet and the other inside the crown. Figures II and III illustrate how the brim should look when completed.

We now turn to the crown, which consists of one-half yard of black velvet draped in soft folds. To drape the crown, commence with the two points at the direct back. First take one end of the velvet, fold in the selvedge edge, measure seven inches and double it; this forms one point. Take the other side of the velvet, measure eight inches, double in the same manner, then sew to the back of the bonnet. Figure II show the position of the points. Allow the velvet to assume natural folds, and turn in the raw edge and slipstitch it to the fancy strip. One end of the velvet forms an end at the left side-back; a small piece of velvet makes the cross knot.

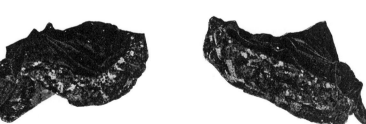

FIGURE I

FIGURE III

CHILD'S ONE-PIECE CAP OR BONNET

A BONNET IN ONE PIECE, No. 7599, COM-
POSED OF LAWN AND LACE INSERTION,

In launder-
ing, the bonnet is drawn out on the cords
as shown in the illustration.   A frill of
lace affords an edge finish, and rosettes

7599—CHILD'S ONE-PIECE CAP OR BONNET.

of ribbon on top render the cap generally becoming.   Ribbon ties are used.
Pattern 7599 is in 5 sizes, infants, ½
yr., 1 yr., 2 yrs. and 3 years.   For 1 year,
it calls for ½ yard 20 inches wide, or ⅜
yard 36 inches wide.   Price, 10 cents.

Additional Instructions For 7599

Use 1/4" seams. Match stars of
Brim and Crown together; insert
1/2" wide lace between the two
layers; sew together; turn right-side-
out; top-stitch 3/16" in from seam
to form casing. Lay 1/2" wide lace
on right side of triangle edge of
Crown; sew together; turn right-
side-out; top-stitch 3/16" in from
edge to form casing. Narrowly hem
each center back edge. Turn and
hem front and neck edges; stitch
lace to these edges. Stitch lace, ribbon ties, two tiny buttons and two
button loops as illustrated. Make a
small hole at each end of the two
casings and insert a heavy crochet
thread into each. Pull each thread
tight on the wrong side of bonnet
and tie into a bow; button the two
buttons and place on doll's head.
Will fit a 9-1/2" doll's head size.

★ #7599 Crown fold ◄

★ #7599 Brim Fold front center back neck edge

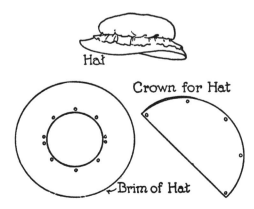

9250, CHILDREN'S CAP (SOMETIMES CALLED THE "EASY TO LAUNDER" BONNET). Described on this page.

9250–CHILDREN'S CAP.

This dainty little cap is made of sheer white nainsook, and trimmed with embroidered edging and insertion. It is sometimes called the "Easy to Launder" bonnet, as the unfastening at the side and back portions permit the bonnet to be spread open and easily ironed. The cap consists of a plain front piece trimmed with narrow bands, and back and side portions cut in one and attached to the front piece. The lower edge of the back is laid in a scant box plait and finished with a narrow band. The sides are plaited at the lower edges and finished with bands. When the bonnet is arranged for wear, the back edges of the sides are joined by a small strap piece and buttons and buttonholes. The back portion is buttoned to the lower edges of the side portions, as indicated. Strings are attached to the forward edges.

Nainsook, dimity, lawn, linen, organdy, chambray, all-over lace, all-over embroidery or China silk may be used to develop this design, with lace insertion, embroidered edging or beading to trim.

The Delineator   1909

Instructions For Pattern Below

Pin Crown to Brim, matching dots. Run a gathering stitch around the crown, pins still in place. Stitch in place. Lining is optional.

Hat

Crown for Hat

Brim of Hat

Lil and

And Their Stylishly

By MRS. OLIVER

Lena

Dressed Dolls

BELL BUNCE

ALL THREE HAD A SEWING BEE OUT IN THE ORCHARD

LIL and LENA were first cousins who lived in a pretty village just out of the big city of New York and had homes opposite each other on the same street. Lil opening her front door cried out, "Lena! Lena! come over and let's go up in the sewing-room and make our dolls some new spring hats." Lena walked slowly over and in a low voice said : "Lil, I never could make a doll's hat." "Of course you never can, Lena, if you don't try. I think girls like us of eight or ten should find the way to dress our own dolls. You go upstairs and I will be there in a minute." Into the sewing-room the little girls went. Lil, the elder of the two, knew in a certain closet on a certain nail on the right-hand side hung a big old-fashioned piece bag with bits of silk and satin, Swiss and muslins bulging out on all sides and of every tint imaginable, which nimble fingers could work into beautiful garments for these much cherished bran-new dolls.

"Oh, Lena, isn't that lovely !" and the enthusiastic Lil held it up before her, her face beaming with delight. "What will it make? Oh! I know, a dear, sweet poke sunbonnet. Here is just the way you cut it out, an oval piece for the crown and a rounding piece for the rim."

A Stylish Straw Hat

"That will be too dear for anything. You see, Lena, the crown is big and fits nicely into the rim, which is striped with lace." "But Lil, they are not alike." "Well, goosey, what difference does that make ?" "They form the front, and this lace will lie against Margery's dear face," which was Lil's own doll. "Now, Lena, what will we do for ribbons to tie the bonnet? Oh! I recollect, mamma put in the top bureau drawer a piece of baby-blue satin just the thing for this spring hat."

The little girls set to work with a will to see which one would succeed best. Lena knew that unless she was very spry she would be left far behind. Said Lil in a cheery tone, "I love to make a doll's hat. Every one of my dolls shall have one of these except Louisa ; she is too old for such a young bonnet, as you know she is the mother of my five little children."

Looking up archly, tapping Lil on the shoulder, Lena said : "You are a queer child, but I love you because you are my cousin and you know more than I do about bonnets, and even if I am stupid I know something very nice and very pretty. Suppose we make two garden hats, lingerie hats mamma calls them, out of crinkle tissue-paper; mamma's got some she did not use for the parlor shade. Your Bessie would look

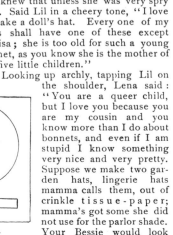

A Smart Tam-O'-Shanter

lovely in blue, while my Clara would be sweet in pink. Our dollies would be the envy of the street, but be sure not to tell the Thomson girls how they are made. We will make them on Saturday or to-morrow after school."

This clever idea was eagerly snapped up by the industrious Lil, and in a few days the garden hats bloomed forth proudly, showing themselves up and down on both sides of the attractive village street, the neighbors children gazing with wonder and admiration at the beautiful creations. These lingerie hats were made by taking a round piece of crêpe paper and then cutting another narrow strip of the paper, doubling it in the middle and pulling out the crinkles carefully so that both edges formed a ruffle, then gathering this onto the center and hiding the join by a band of ribbon. A ribbon bow in the front and ribbon ties complete this Paris creation.

Before the week was over the whole village made garden hats and poke sunbonnets, so our little girls declared they could not allow their dolls to wear anything so common, and as Lil and Lena had become the arbiters of doll's fashions, a more quiet head covering was substituted; and their aunt, who was an expert in the millinery trade, invented a tam-o'-shanter made of red cloth and one day brought them home two pretty doll's straw hats and trimmed both with feathers that came out of her favorite Cochin-China's tail.

By this time the dollies' millinery had become so fine that Lil and Lena decided that they positively must have some new clothes. So they invited their little friend Edith White to come over almost every fine afternoon, and all three had a sewing bee out in the orchard, and before long the dollies were stylishly attired.

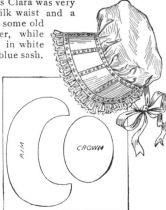

A Lingerie Effect

Lil made her doll Bessie a pretty dress of pink lawn from a piece that was left from a dress her aunt had made last year. And Lena's Clara was very stylishly attired in a blue silk waist and a white cloth skirt made from some old pieces that were given her, while Edith dressed her doll all in white Swiss finished with a smart blue sash.

Now if every little girl who reads this will follow the diagrams on this page given for a guide in cutting out the tam and the sunbonnet, and will use the McCall Patterns illustrated on page 301 of McCall's Magazine for December for her dollies' clothes, she will have no more difficulty than Lil and Lena had in making their doll children the most stylish in the town.

A Dainty Sunbonnet

DOLL'S FIVE-GORE HAT

Additional Instructions

Cut five gores from lightweight wool, velvet or cotton and one bias strip brim (2" x 9-3/4") from contrasting material such as silk or 2" wide ribbon. Sew each gore side seam (3/16" seam) together; press. Hat may be lined with a thin material at this point. With the wrong side of bias strip together, press strip in half lengthwise. With bias strip on wrong side of hat, pin and sew raw seams (3/16" seams) together; blind-stitch raw ends of strip together. Turn strip up onto right side of hat. Finish with a ribbon rosette and feather if desired. Will fit a doll's 9-1/2" head size.

368   368

Set 368 consists of a coat, dress and gored hat; and for a doll twenty-four inches tall one yard of material thirty-six inches wide will be required for the coat; five-eights of a yard thirty-six inches wide for the dress, with one-quarter of a yard of contrasting material thirty-six inches wide for the collar, cuffs and belt. The coat and hat are equally attractive.

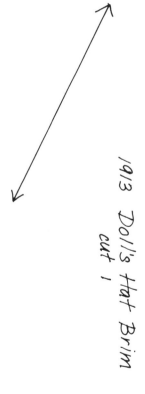

1913 Doll's Hat Brim
cut 1

1913 Doll's Hat
cut 5

Designs to Meet Every Doll Need

Girl Dolls' Set 4783

Girl Dolls' Set 5413

Girl Dolls' Dress 4856

Girl Dolls' Redingote Costume 5967

Girl Dolls Set 4221

4221—This cunning little dress is intended for girl dolls, and has body and sleeves in one, with straight side-plaited skirt. Rompers are included. Dolls' Set No. 4221, sizes for 18, 20, 22 and 24-inch dolls. The 22-inch size requires for dress 1⅛ yard 36-inch material, ⅞ yard for rompers. Price, 10 cents.

4783—Two dresses are provided in this set for girl dolls—a one-piece dress cut in one with short sleeves, and a middy dress. Dolls' Set No. 4783, sizes for 16, 18, 20, 22, 24, 26, 28 and 30-inch dolls. Size 20 requires for one-piece dress 1⅛ yard 27-inch material; for middy dress, 1¼ yard 27-inch material. Price, 10 cents.

5413—A complete street outfit for a girl doll is provided in this set, which includes a smart French dress, a coat and a hat. Dolls' Set No. 5413, sizes for 14, 16, 18, 20, 22, 24, 26, 28 and 30-inch dolls. Size 18 requires ⅞ yard 27-inch material for dress, ⅞ yard for coat, and ¼ yard for hat. Price, 10 cents.

4856—Below a round yoke, this dress is tucked front and back, and is cut in one with the sleeves. No. 4856, sizes for 16, 18, 20, 22, 24, 26, 28 and 30-inch dolls. Size 20 requires ⅞ yard 27-inch material. Price, 10 cents.

5967—Just like Mother's redingote costume is this, the redingote arranged over a foundation dress of satin cut in one with long sleeves. Dolls' Redingote Costume No. 5967, sizes for 14, 16, 18, 20, 22, 24, 26, 28 and 30-inch dolls. Size 22 requires ½ yard 44-inch serge, ⅞ yard 36-inch satin including hat. Price, 10 cents.

5406—A smart dress for dolly is shown, made with sleeves and long waist in one. A hat is included. Dolls' Set No. 5406, sizes for 14, 16, 18, 20, 22, 24, 26, 28 and 30-inch dolls. Size 18 requires ⅞ yard 36-inch material. Price, 10 cents.

5410—Very dear to the little mother's heart is the baby doll, and this set of clothes will keep the little darling properly clothed. Set No. 5410, sizes for 14, 16, 18, 20, 22, 24, 26, 28 and 30-inch dolls. Size 18 requires for dress 1½ yard, for coat 1 yard, and for cap ⅜ yard 27-inch material. Price, 10 cents. Embroidery 11742, transfer pattern, 15 cents.

(Descriptions continued on Page 57)

Girl Dolls' Dress and Hat 5406

Lady Dolls' Dress 5360

Lady Dolls' Coat 5362

Infant Dolls' Set 5410

Girl Dolls' Dutch Set 5920

Boy Dolls' Dutch Set 5920

Dolls' Set 5938

Girl Dolls' Set 5938

Lady Dolls' Dress 4823

For a complete assortment of Designs see THE FASHION BOOK, WINTER NUMBER: for sale at all Pictorial Review Pattern Agencies at 25 cents a copy including one pattern—by mail 35 cents from The Pictorial Review Company, New York.

DOLLS' HATS FROM CRAPE PAPER.

CUT the paper crosswise in strips. These strips should be from one-half inch to an inch in width, according to the fineness of the braid desired. Pin three of them to a cushion in front of you, and braid them. Make the first three

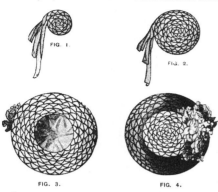

FIG. 1.   FIG. 2.

FIG. 3.   FIG. 4.

strips of uneven length by cutting off an inch from one, and two inches from another, so that the joining will not come at the same place.

When you have braided as far as you can, and are ready to add new strips, do not sew or paste them together, but fold the ends of the new strips for about an inch into the ends of the strips already braided. That is the only difficult part of the work, but you will soon learn to do the joining skilfully.

Begin to sew at the same end of the braid where you began to braid, and make the center of the crown by forming a small, round loop of the braid. Work round to the left, setting the braid with one of its edges under the edge of the previous row. (Fig. 1.) Keep the work perfectly flat, holding the braid in the left hand, and sewing with a short stitch on top, and a long one underneath.

The size of the doll's head will determine the number of rows you will need for the top of the crown. When you think the top is large enough, draw the braid tighter with the left hand, and keep on sewing. Fig. 2 shows how the braid begins to narrow, as in crochet work. Turn it down to make the side of the crown. Four or five rows done in that manner usually form a crown of sufficient height.

Now comes the brim. Do not cut the braid, but simply turn it back on the crown,—right sides together,—and overcast the edges for one whole round. Then flatten out your one row of brim and proceed toward the left as before, keeping the edge of the braid under the edge of the previous row. When the brim is wide enough, cut the braid and fasten it carefully on the under side; the hat part is then complete.

If the trimming is to be sewed to the brim at any place, it must be put on before the hat is faced. Forget-me-nots or other small flowers are charming when combined with a twist of chiffon or silk round the crown. Fig. 4 shows an attractive trimming.

The hats must all be faced to hide the long stitches underneath the brim. The facing — usually of net, chiffon, or silk—can be cut to fit, and put on plain or shirred. If it is to be shirred, make the strip one and a half times as long as the distance round the outer edge of the brim. In sewing on the facing, use a "slip" stitch, and be careful that you do not sew entirely through either the braid or the shirred silk facing.

Cut a lining of the same material as the facing, and make the strip just long enough to go round the inside of the crown. Sew the lining into the crown, and your work is finished.

Hot Weather Hats for Every Doll

Baby blue with pink rosebuds—for your youngest

DO YOU ever think of keeping your doll children cool and comfortable these hot days? The new summer hats for dolls are made of paper, just ordinary crêpe paper. They are very easy to make, too, and any little girl can fit out her whole family in an afternoon.

To make any one of the hats on this page, cut three strips of crêpe paper one and one-half inches wide, pull out the crimp so that the paper will appear smooth, and braid tightly. These hats are made over a patty or a custard cup. First cover the cup with a piece of crêpe paper about twelve inches square, tucking the excess paper inside the cup to hold it in place. Place the cup bottom side up upon a table, and coat the paper covering with thick paste (not mucilage).

Beginning at the center of the crown, press the braided paper firmly to the pasted paper on the cup, running the braid round and round until the crown is complete.

Pull out the paper which has been tucked inside the cup and allow it to spread out upon the table. Cover it with paste and continue running the braided paper around until a large-enough brim has been formed. Use the table as a support while pressing on the braid and allow the hat to dry partially before removing it from the cup.

The hat in the upper left-hand corner is of light blue with a wreath of pink, yellow and black roses, and green leaves. The roses are made from a half-inch strip of crêpe paper rolled to form the petals, which are then pasted tightly to the hat. The leaves are cut from green paper.

The hat in the upper right-hand corner of the page is of yellow crêpe paper and trimmed with blue corn flowers, made by twisting a half-inch strip of crêpe paper, gathering it up in loops and tying tightly in the center.

The hat on the little vacation doll has a lilac-colored crown with a white brim. The plume is from a strip of white fringed crêpe paper.

Each of the hats measures two and a half inches across the inside of the crown.   MILDRED AUSTIN SHINN.

"Good-by," she waves, off for a vacation in her smart traveling hat of lilac and white

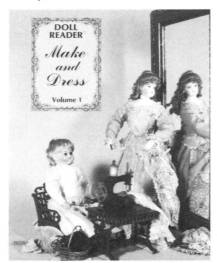